Being Us

Shakti Shankar Dandapat

ISBN 978-93-5610-660-4

Published in India 2022 by Pencil

A brand of
One Point Six Technologies Pvt. Ltd.
123, Building J2, Shram Seva Premises,
Wadala Truck Terminal, Wadala (E)
Mumbai 400037, Maharashtra, INDIA
E connect@thepencilapp.com
W www.thepencilapp.com

Author biography

Shakti Shankar Dandapat studied in Utkal University, Bhubaneswar and The English and Foreign Languages University, Hyderabad, India. His doctoral research is on Odia Poetry in English. His first two books of poems in English are entitled "Out of Nothingness" and "Achintya". He is an Assistant Professor in the P.G. Department of English at Maharaja Sriram Chandra Bhanjadeo University (erstwhile North Orissa University), Baripada, Odisha.

CONTENTS

Preface

Being Us strives to be the voice of people who are at peace with themselves. Grateful for blessings. Aware of frailties. Grounded, compassionate and empathetic. They who aspire to attaining the joy within. They are on a quest – seeking answers to questions like "Who am I?" "Why am I the way I am?" etc. The questions offer them fulfilment rather than the vague irritation of confronting questions. Answers to questions such as these tempt us towards them but leave us fulfilled without them. Because the healthiest kind of sense of being we can achieve is probably through self understanding and inner peace. We are all perfect human beings the moment we accept everyone including us the way we are. We regret, repent and thereby redeem and recreate ourselves. Lifelong.

Being us teases us towards becoming us…

Acknowledgements

Dedicated to

My parents, Mr/s. Ramormila Dandapat, for teaching me love, compassion, and life's values. My wife, Mamali. My son, Achintya Krishiv Kalyan Dandapat and my dear student, Alpha(Lamealphaaz).

Grateful to

My teachers, friends, relatives, students and above all, my readers.

Bless Thee

Bless thy body to bear thy pain
For scars are the adornments of the weird and insane
No rest for the wicked
He doth not slumber
No love for the evil
He hath none for the giving
You feel no chill in the air as the blades rotate
He is not one to easy breathe
Clouded judgement makes dirty deeds
For every sinners or righteousness
There is a forever sleep.

Lines Of Green

The sky darkens
Lines of green the colour of red
Run the path of nothing dead
The air is pissed white
With the groans of lion's limbs
Glistening irises march to the tune
Of that which smoulders
There are no strangers to this smoggy city
Lilies are no strangers to this smoggy city
Lilies of the field clothed
Birds of the air He feeds
An inch not added
It be the kingdom ye the lost must seek
Slipping the castle becomes the bishop
Gallantry murders thy troops
Heavy lies the lids that keep
Sudden is the zephyr the current change
Alight embers freeze
It was inevitable the rain descends.

Can You Hear

Can You Hear ???
Can you hear the wind ?
Do you hear its song ?
The song of the burning forests and all children she lost
Children she lost to fire to the land's creature
The fire that consumes all without mercy
The fire of inhumanity within the humans
And the blade that marks all with destructions
Mercy that men sing of the mouth of death
Death that forgets not and forgives all
The inhumanity you too should take.

When The Pages Sing

Like a kite flying high I see no strings
Holding my time with closed eyes
I tell harmless lies to the giggling wind
As it pushes me in the endless sky
I trade this space with empty pockets
Gathering and squandering
Healing and riffling
Staying on my toes for the passers-by
Who walks an extra mile
Just to be by my side
Aware of the plight
That fervently disavows
Digressing the course of flight
Write long songs
Pitched on high highs and low lows
Never falling flat on ears
That pages enclose.

Hope

Hope abounds in morning dew drops
Freshness in brought by season's raindrops
Why do you mope so dear heart
When ambition is shown
By snow capped mountain tops
New day brings a fresh new start
Sunrise plays the centralising part
Why do you worry, dear heart
When brilliance is shown by clouds painting art
Blooming flower buds bring new life
Trees show to live without strife
Why do you pine so dear heart
When freedom is shown
By a majestic bird's flight
Nature teaches lessons of living
It teaches compassion and power of giving
Why do you not learn dear heart
When love is shown by life on earth.

Disguised

With the bleeding distal phalange
I tied the knots of our disguised
Hearts in such away
That it would never slither.

Butterfly

Ghoulish phantoms
Stab the amber butterfly
Resting on my forehead
While my demons dance
In my hollow chest
A cold shiver down the spine
And an inferno in the heart
I helplessly carry in me a madness within
With a quiet demeanour
Is this duplicity ?
Or just layers to being a human ?

Ways that die

The melting point of rainbows
The strength of horizons
I lose myself in soft eyes
And find me in pieces
Scattered in fields of stones
Perhaps the ropes of a hauling
Broke, and knotted rainbows had to die
Perhaps the horizon came apart
In the fading light of a dusk
There must be redemption
An escape from those eyes
A thousand stones can not cover me
Nor my fragments be stitched together
In a patchwork guilt of tomorrows
The rest of dusk is darkness
And wicked whispers of wandering winds
As I cast aside my vestments of all before
All hereafter lies untied
Soft eyes and knotted rainbows
Horizons that held fast against the tide
A candle fights the lonesome alone
It is just the ways that die.

Knots

Knots knotsknots
Twisting and tangling and tweaking and stretching
I feel them inside my gut
As date's deft fingers
Untie the silvery strings
Attached to my dreams
I see them around my hands
Fastening them tight
As the societal norms
Discord with my own
I choke and what do you know
Knots in my larynx drown
My views and opinions
And bury them deep down
My feet get entangled
With fifty other sets
And for reasons I know not
They get knotted bound.

Parallel Worlds

Parallel worlds
Look and long to find enclosure
Just beyond the horizon
In the merging of
Their parallel thinking

The Alter

I trembled before the alter
My dreams crying at my feet
The looming face of reality
Calmly sipping tea
I tripped and stuttered
Spilled uncooked words on nothing
For all eyes to see
I was scared
I shivered at nights
Stuffing tears under secrecy
Because the house grew colder
And colder like hell frozen around me
I attempted to hide
The way I shook
Rooted to the spot
Where I would either rise or fall
I was scared.

Forever Is A Lie

Forever is a lie, isn't it ?
But wrapped in the dearth of present
To collide somewhere again down the line
With a promise to fill the cracks
By washing off the lies chilling the bones
While signifying to navigate the waters of life
Without demoralising the good instincts one holds
Whilst flooding one's face with perplexed emotions at once
Minutes after picturing everything in the head
But as time goes on everything gets messed up
And when one tries to catch those moments
Soon gets evaporated by finding another house to dwell in.

Echoes

I heard your voice echoing in my head
Scattered like the moon on the blistering surface of an ocean
Festering inside me as crashing softly around my heart
Allow tides of my love to drag that softly through corners
And plant it on my skin
At least it'd be visible
Would you dare to glance through
Let me be a snow flake then
Atleast I can travel with slow winds
And freeze to silence
To experience the beauty of aurora
To weave new ways towards my dreams
And spiral down gradually into my own aura
By leaving you behind.

On Sadness

I could tell you that
Sadness is a full grown tree that has never seen any end
That it is those unsold wilting marigolds that the flower seller takes back home everyday
I could tell you that the confronted patriarchy and
The prospect of new life
That is a home with boarded windows
And mildew covered walls
I could clothe sadness with pages of poetry
To make it prettier
To make it's presence in the corner of your mind
And a little more bearable while so pathetic
Sadness is, in reality, a gaping wound that is
Too raw for me to bandage with anything
Only poetry heals.

Like Water

I am water
A shapeless structure
Knowing my importance
I remain one with the earth
From the air inhaled
To the tides in the sea
I remain the same
Evolving forms constantly
Untamed elements withstanding any climate
Indestructible creation
The clash amongst the titans
Abused in wasteful manners
As fee see I am vital
Taking for granted daily
Be ware I destroy every rival.

The Heaven Is Burning

My heaven is burning in rage
In rage of me numbing to my pain
Numbness makes you stay
Stay in a place
A place that wants to get rid of you
But you are stubborn enough to
Wear any ragged rigor
Stains on the wall over yourself
To hide your shame
Shame residing in every sweat pore
Every hair follicle that comes out
Only when you try to stand
On your feet with a bravery so frail
That you ultimately fall on your face
I am a hell turned to an insane sage
Performing on a live stage
I am mortified in my skin
Lacking coherence in my mind
Looking into the mirror before
Trading my soul
My grief doesn't recognise me anymore.

A Voice

All are tired except my clock
As it's still counting each hour
Most eyes are tightly shut
Seems as dead
While the owls on branches
Look depressed
With their eyes open wide
Trying to find something
In the darkness of night
Night painted black singing
Serene lullabies
But my disenchanted soul only
Listening haunting screams
A voice of tortured my ears
It's the roaring of my hidden fears
Fear quite similar to a shape shifter
Who have numerous shapes
Will never know what would be next
Thought makes my heart shiver
The idea of losing someone
Sometimes freezes my soul
Thinking death standing before
Makes my throat choke
An image of laughing people
Holds my steps back

Thinking about failure
All dreams get packed
What if I get deserted by most
Loving ones when I think
Try to exchange my heart into
A stiff store
As fear has countless masks
Changes so fast
Fears are like nightmares
Seen with open eyes
As fears are fearless
Often haunt at night
But doesn't mean they are scared off
Bright daylight.

I Walk

Tensile stress and tensile strength
To reach you I walk on a thin fragile scope
Taking each counted step
Measuring foot length of love
With every step
The love seems grave deep
A step and a falter
And it breaks
An added weight
And I tumble
Sweat and breath
Both run out
But I walk I walk
I walk a line of fragile hope.

Hope In Vain

Filthy days
Ushered with pain
I remembered how I grew hope in vain
Some days won't be jocund
I know though
But unfiltered smile
Tired eyes peeps into
The past yet so.

Waves

When the tide goes out to sea
And leaves the sand on shore to me
I sit and stare thoughts long and deep
Thoughts that we in seashells keep
Solitude converges from the sea and sky
Sand and salt
My thoughts and I
I fill the darkness with the fragrance of the sea
And my soul fills a shore far away from me
Can hear all the silence that I contain
And lights of lamps call for me in vain
There was once a footprint here beneath the foam
I pick up its remains and leave for home.

Seekers

Those who seek desire in the lure of night
Often find themselves embracing the sunshine
Washing away regret in hopes of semblance
Often leaves them stranded midway
Those who seek forgiveness in lullabies
Often reek of deception and disguise
Alas! It holds true to me and you
Often withholding get wondering why ?

Poetries

Festoon your aura with optimism
Flying high above with giggles
Accepting rather than expecting
And letting go of the ephemeral pain
Etch your pessimism with beauty
And pour out your worries
Throw them in the world of despair
And land into the plain of poetries.

The Rising Dawn

Never have I seen the darkest night
Snuff the lamp of a rising dawn
As I lay in bed thinking
I feel myself sinking
Deep in thought while excavating
A set of stars on the scoop
Different colour one by one
Yet remained in a group
Each tree coated in mahogany like lungs to the human body
Which serve a similar function here on mother earth
What a gift it is being able to breath upon birth
Since all things are compromised of atoms
Do we really even exist ?
An atom is made out of empty space
For me that's no sigh of a trace.

The Unsung Songs

I wished to be your unsung poetry
Infused and disguised
Your ocean of infinite words
Curled by the rhythm of life and me
Your expound prosody
Singing the syllables of idioms and phrases
Touching your lips
Soft and deep
Your sonnet swaying
Metaphor and smiles of all odds and evens
I be gifting the woods of eternity.

Screams

I grow weary of listening to the screams
They never leave
I am tired of the hurting
It never stops
I am tired of having to watch people turn monsters
Or is it monsters that turn into people ?
These days oh I don't know
Those words ring in my head
They kill each other with their love
So hatred only stay.

Life Is A Game

Vulnerable cries of children and women
Amid men's thunderstorms
Mother's embrace hopeless
In the misty smoke of terror
Peace fades from brotherhood of nations
And hid in the debris of hostilities
Thirst and hunger
For blood trends and trades
Like a favourite sport
In the fabulous arena
Contrived spectators
With life's sanctity games are played.

Destiny Or Slavery

You led me out of my Egypt
And held back every sea of iniquity
For my destiny is not held captive to slavery
But is held for eternity in your promised land
You led me through the heated wastelands
And got me through every problem I ever had
Forever I remember the exodus of my heart
And how happy I wad led to you
So happy that sometimes I feel sad.

Harmless Lies

Like a kite flying high
I see no strings
Holding my time with closed eyes
I tell harmless lies to the giggling wind
As it pushes me in the endless sky
I trade this space with empty pockets
Gathering and squandering
Healing and riffling
Staying on my toes for the passer by
Who walks an extra mile
Just to be my side
Aware of the plight
That fervently disavows
Disagreeing the course of flight
I write love songs
Pitched on high highs and low lows
Never falling flat on ears
That pages enclose.

Belongings

He went to the forest where he feels he belongs
Striding through debris and hopping over logs
The skeletons of the leafless trees
Veins pumping darkness into the sunset
Cliff face before him
He wishes he could fly
Spotting a boulder he pushes it from
The cliff face and watches it break
Through every way on the way down
He found serenity in such destruction
Sometimes destructions be so beautiful
As the way mind wants.

A Fading Light

I am but a fading light
Set upon a path
To learn to teach
To receive and give
From birth till death
It's what we are
Each breath given for that never lasts
So up and rise
Stay still
And show the world
You are still alive.

Masterpieces

When its over
And can be mended never
When it's beyond control
Hands too weak to hold
When its forever broken
And all dusted and done
When hope is gone
Left forlorn
I blessed you to turn to the one
The expert of redemption
And the lord of restoration
Who with broken pieces makes masterpieces
And changes the trajectories for the stories
Is anything beyond control
For the commander of all ?

Peace

Now as the bells ring
The darkness feels like sunlight on my face
Soft, silent, sad night wrapped in the silk of a moth
Hold these seeds in your palms
Hold them in your fists
Forget them in your pockets
And grow back as sunflowers
When you fall into your open tombs
On this soil
Oh your ancestor's land
So you so yearn to cherish
When the voices are gone.

Hymns

The fly on the mirror chants
Like the magician in chains
Thin veil, repent, and repetition
The lady in the box never disappear
But you might be surprised what comes next.

Glow Like The Leaden Moon

I stretch tangled in the winter mood sheets
Grow taller than the dethroned stems of dried roses
Dust floats effortlessly
But the clouds next to a pearl white sun
They float lighter than a hummingbird feather
Do you notice anything familiar ?
Starring too long into the sun
Patterns appear and they dance and come alive
In that spot where a sphere of fire used to be
I manifest a pack of honey bad gems
As the sun pours down my face
Billowing on the dove liner
I swallow the sun
And glow like the leaden moon
I glow as the way I want

To Kill Us All

Resources getting lower
Stake claim invisible borders
Ownership chains
Rights to their survival
Hush hush
The allies alibis
Benefit the side
That sustains you also
What about the kids
You robbed of a future
Deployed to heaven
Tears of realisation
They are never coming back
All to gain more oil and gas
I hope your food source is safe
From the nuclear wasteland
Under the dark clouds of grey
Cancerous growth of hate and greed
Just think
That nuclear bomb was meant to kill us all
We lay holding hand
Begging for no more bloodshed
On the frozen floor
Of the fallout shelter
Clinging to our prayers.

Wars

Wars will get end soon
But not the waiting of a child
For his martyred father
Wars will get end soon
But not the waiting of a wife
For his beloved husband
Wars will get end soon
But not the waiting of a mother

Teary Eyes

There is mess
Bodies lying everywhere
Hopes scattered
Teary eyes
Pool of blood and scary scenes
The disasters make us numb
The hatred and bitterness
There is no end no start
The same old war

Agony

I wish to ink my agony
But poetry needs to be subtle
After all love is cruel
Wicked and mostly helpless
Knowing my soul is timid
My quill is the reflection of her very own soul
So tell me how I am supposed
To ink death note when
Love happens to be pure and marvel.

My Downfall

Look at me
Relishing the thoughts of my downfall
Floating around in my mind
Like demonic butterflies and angelic moths
Never banish them
For I know not how to
The vital gear inside of me
Producing that will to preserve
Ran it's last course long age
And in a terrifying way profound yet
So lost.

Still Standing

Above the brume
Fir forests vivid in their stillness
Stand singing
Praising the otherness
Of world at night
And stars rejoice
In this realm
Where soul is alive

The Touch Of Love

When the moon finally
Came out of clouds
Stars started appearing with glittery shine
A breeze passed out
Leaving the touch of love
She finally opened
The diary had written
A poetry of confusion
Since long time but that beautiful ambience
Made her to recite those lines
And with the end of the poetry there began
A story forever.

The Face I Hide

Roaming among the judging minds
I see the running races trying
To earn the graves that will shine
But the muffled bells are waiting
To echo their farewell sounds
So well that the fate is re-destined
Maybe someday I will flirt with the flirting time
In the bivouac of life
To say to not to trust future
No matter how finely designed
But to act act now act today
But to live live now live today
To make our lives sublime
For every new tomorrow speaks
How the old today is dying
Darkness inside darkness outside
I find myself darkened
May the face I hide
Will signify the humanly deeds so divine
Hearts within the houses
Houses within the hearts
And the forlorn travellers
May you labor and wait
Wait and labor

So a peaceful path
Your desired restless feet will find.

For When A Star Falls

For when a star falls
It falls alone
I see the shining sun crying crying like a lone
For the bright day soon will come
And the significance of the moon will be gone
Oh those those broken forgotten dreams
Within this skin and bone
Welcome to your same old new home
Maybe those unilluminated
Brown eyes are forlorn
Though the rivers of tears
Will bring back the greeny songs
May be I am falling and falling
Though this fall will inspire millions
The world oh my my dear world
Let the weak will be strong
Maybe I have a sleeping tongue
For when I
I will be gone
The sky will be full of wind and stones
As within these words
I hide I hide
Storms

Homely

You watch that face
You see these eyes
You looking over those curls
You go gaga at that smile
It's the unknown street
But it feels so homely
Following it blindly
Yes that voice is so sweet
It happens to be crossroads further
I believe they have a destiny
But have no idea whether me and she ever meet if
It's that heart feels so inclined towards her
That no words could brief
O' the mistress of heaven
Get me a hope
To the masters of love
I have promises to keep.

Crimson Ink

He took a fist sized mass
Connected it with veins and nerves
Innervated in arteries
Coloured in crimson ink
Injected adrenaline and nor adrenaline
It started beating rhythmically in his subject
He
The subject had a heart only for beating
He was the God
Some people have heart only for living
If he existed so can others be.

Paper & Pen

The masochistic blank paper begged the sadistic pen
To choke it with the words that broke the mind
So much feelings inside
Yet not enough life
A one way screaming match
Between the mind and the heart
One is bound to be quiet
So the mind beautifully lies to the heart
That the way of life
At that anointed horizons
Where the dawn meets the dark
This innate respire got entwined
To eminent oratorical hymns
The desiccated despondency
Get started to thrive from these
Inchoate moments of veneration.

One Memory Away

I went by the spirals today
Alone and intruded they felt
One memory away
Knight of my bad day
The laughter through the pain
Left me stripped
With every echo
My walls down
Bruised and invaded
My mind torn
My heart ground
Another roll
I need to be numb .

Solitude Is Mine

In the light
I quest for darkness
To gaze at the twinkling stars
In the crowd
I quest for isolation
To embrace my deserted scars
In the sunshine
I quest for rain
To saturate my blistering soul
In this fast city life
I quest for myself
I seek peace
I pine for myself
In my lowest in my deepest
In my darkest nights

Mahjabeen

I have seen many dreams
I have trapped the vast sky
With the thin little strings
The sun haunts my mind
Though a peaceful soul the moon will bring
Beloved you need not trade all your bells
Just to signify the noisy hollow rings
Good bye to the life you used to live
And the world you used to know
For there's coming a new script
With the big brand screen
Alas one pays a bitter price of truth
So the liars will stand near the chapel
Oh they stand so firm
The dear deary world worldly mess
Where I used to try to fit in
And now I no more desire to be here
Within the poor folks and their rich siblings
Myself I hold
So tight I hold
And run and run
And there are very few who will mind.

Stand & Sing

Why you left your dear world
Are you afraid of your created thing
Or for the very perfection of being
We call them angels
Are they just your guards with maleficent wings
Tell me where you dwell
So I may stand and sing
I find the very reflection of yours
Within every living being
Oh but the clever you
You add pain so everytime they laugh
It will sting
And chaos within
Show me the facts that your existence is divine
In your name religion they attacks
Playing with the innocent minds
Why did you create and hide
The perfect design the perfect concept
Yet why are you so shy
Show us the way to your home
So there the trust may begin
There is no rich no poor in the sky above
Though they divide the earth below
Heavy so heavy the clothes are
Yet the bodies are hollow

You and you and you
They talk they think they seek
The very you
The fake even the true
If you are here or there or anywhere
Give them strength oh Lord
So they may complete
The circle of their divine feeling.

www.ingramcontent.com/pod-product-compliance
Lightning Source LLC
LaVergne TN
LVHW050422160726
843469LV00041B/1201

* 9 7 8 9 3 5 6 1 0 6 6 0 4 *